C000075850

OFFSIDE?
UGH!

Written by Lindsay & Seth Little

Illustrated by Daniel Gill

Meyer & Meyer Sport

British Library Cataloguing in Publication Data

A catalogue record for this book is available from the British Library

Offsides? Ugh!

All rights reserved, especially the right to copy and distribute, including the translation rights. No part of this work may be reproduced—including by photocopy, microfilm or any other means—processed, stored electronically, copied or distributed in any form whatsoever without the written permission of the publisher.

© 1st Ed. 2016 by LearnSport Books. All rights reserved.
© 2nd Ed. 2016 by LearnSport Books and Meyer & Meyer Sport

Aachen, Auckland, Beirut, Cairo, Cape Town, Dubai, Hägendorf, Hong Kong, Indianapolis, Manila, New Delhi, Singapore, Sydney, Tehran, Vienna

Member of the World Sport Publishers' Association (WSPA)

Manufacturing: Print Consult GmbH, Munich, Germany

ISBN 978-1-78255-097-6
E-Mail: info@m-m-sports.com, service@learnsportbooks.com
www.m-m-sports.com
www.learnsportbooks.com

May 2016

My Life in Soccer

by Yael Averbuch

Soft, green grass. Fun times with my family. Love and joy. Those are some of the first things that come to mind when I think about soccer.

I was seven years old when I watched my first soccer game. I didn't know anything about the sport besides that it seemed fun. My best friend in school invited me to come watch her game and my dad took me to cheer for her. That day, her team needed extra players and they asked me if I would play. I was very shy and said no. After watching her game, though, I decided that it looked like a lot of fun so my dad signed me up to play on a recreational team the next season.

I fell in love with the game at my first soccer practice, and have loved it ever since. It was a special time to share with my dad, as we learned about the game together. It was fun to be out on the field with my teammates and getting to play. And it was a whole new set of skills and experiences that made me very excited to learn.

When I was nine I wrote in my journal that I wanted to be a professional soccer player. I didn't really understand at the time what that meant, and

I certainly didn't know what it would take to get there. But I knew that I wanted to play for as long as I could and be the best I could be.

Since that time, soccer has taken me all across the world. I have played all over the U.S., in England, Germany, Holland, Japan, China, Australia, New Zealand, Thailand, Mexico, Canada, Sweden, Russia, Serbia and many other countries! I have also played for my country. I have formed friendships playing soccer that will last a lifetime. I have also learned a lot about myself through the game. I have learned what it takes to be a champion, and also how to overcome disappointments along the way.

Soccer is called "the beautiful game." There are so many reasons the sport is so beautiful and I'm sure that you will understand them as you play. I love soccer because there is such a variety of skills to learn. There are physical skills (like running fast, being strong, playing aggressively), skills with the ball (dribbling, trapping, shooting), and skills like teamwork and leadership. All are important to the game. There is no one right way to play soccer. It is a game of imagination and creativity.

I am now living the dream I have had since I was nine years old. I am a professional soccer player. It has not always been an easy path to accomplish my goals, but whenever I practice or play, I continue to love soccer more than ever.

Soon after I started playing, my dad and I began a mission to learn the game together. We would watch videos of soccer training and try to do the same drills in my backyard. I hope that you will enjoy learning and practicing the same way I did then, and have continued to do all my career.

I encourage you to learn and play the game of soccer, but most importantly, have fun while you do!

Learn more about Yael Averbuch on her website: www.yaelaverbuch.com Yael is also the founder of the Techne Futbol Training System, which helps players develop the skills necessary to play soccer and have fun: www.technefutbol.com

My name is Alex, and I love to play soccer!

I just started a new soccer season. This year a lot of things seem different.

My team's first game was very strange. When we played soccer last year, there was one referee at each game. He wore a bright yellow shirt and ran all around the field.

This game was different. There were more players on the field, and there were more referees! One referee was in the middle of the

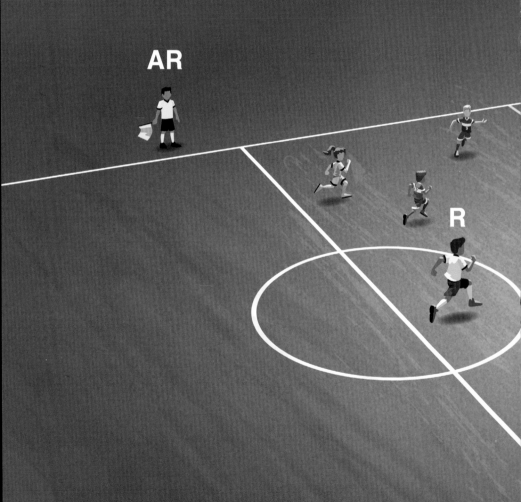

field like last year, and there were two more on the sides of the field. The new referees wore bright shirts and waved yellow flags too.

Coach explained that each referee on the side is called an "Assistant Referee" or "AR." They help the referee in the center of the field watch over the game.

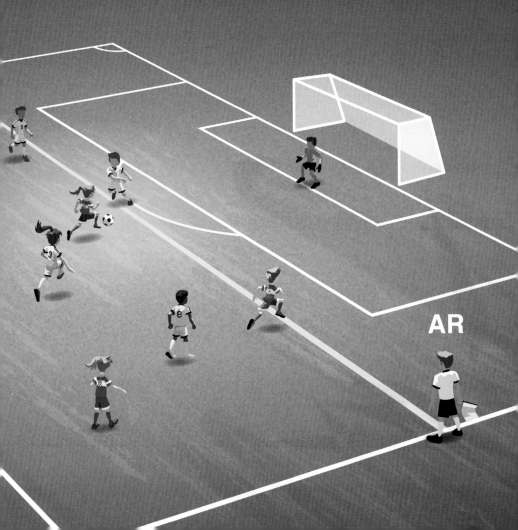

AR

Even though I had fun in our first game, I was really confused by the time the game ended.

Last year the referee only blew his whistle to stop the game when players pushed or tripped each other, when the ball went out of bounds, or if a player touched the ball with his hands.

In this game it seemed like every time we got the ball and raced towards the other team's goal, the assistant referee waved his flag over his head and stuck it out in front of him. Then the referee in the middle blew his whistle, stopped the game, and gave the ball to the other team! We couldn't figure out what was going on. It felt so unfair!

It happened over and over again. My team was frustrated. Some parents even started yelling at the referee. That part was really embarrassing. Each time the referee just calmly said, "You were in an offside position."

Offside? Ugh!

I have to be honest. Even though I had heard the word "offside" before that game, I really didn't know what it meant. That week in practice I asked coach to explain it again.

He said, "If you are standing or running on the field between the other team's last defender and their goal, you are in an 'offside position.' If your teammate tries to pass you the ball, the referee will call an 'offside offense.' You need to make sure you are 'level' with the other team's last defender until the ball is passed forward to you. Then you can race ahead to control it!"

I didn't get it. This whole offside thing was my new least favorite part of the game. It was just too confusing!

In our second game my best friend, Jamie, and I were both playing as forwards. That means we were in the positions nearest the other team's goal trying to create scoring opportunities.

Even though Coach told us at practice that we needed to be "level" with the other team's last defender before our teammates passed the ball to us, it still didn't make any sense.

The referee called offside almost every time Jamie or I got the ball.

During the game, coach quickly tried to explain everything again. This time he talked about being "in front of" and "behind" the other players. Then he talked to some of my teammates about getting "inside" and "outside" and "goal side." Now I was even more confused. Sometimes it feels like coach is speaking a different language! There are so many new soccer words.

At halftime, Coach could tell that we were still confused about this whole offside thing, so he sat us down with a whiteboard to talk more about what being "offside" meant.

He explained that the rule is very difficult to understand and that we didn't need to understand all of it right now. He told us to focus on a few important things.

He said the trick to being onside is to be "level," or side-by-side, with the other team's last defender until the ball is passed forward to me or ahead of me. After the ball is passed forward, I can run to the ball. I can even race ahead of the defender toward his goal. If my teammate controls a pass, then we restart the whole process over again, and I must be level with my teammate or the last defender to be onside.

The referee will only call offside when we pass the ball to one of our teammates that is closer than the other team's defenders to their goal. Coach told us that if we find ourselves closer to the other team's goal than their defenders, we should try and hurry back into an onside position.

Coach drew the other team's players on his whiteboard and showed us where we would be offside. Then we returned to the field early before second half kick, and some of our teammates pretended to be the other team's defenders. Jamie and I practiced staying level with them. No matter where they moved, we made sure we were not closer to their goal than they were until the ball was passed forward.

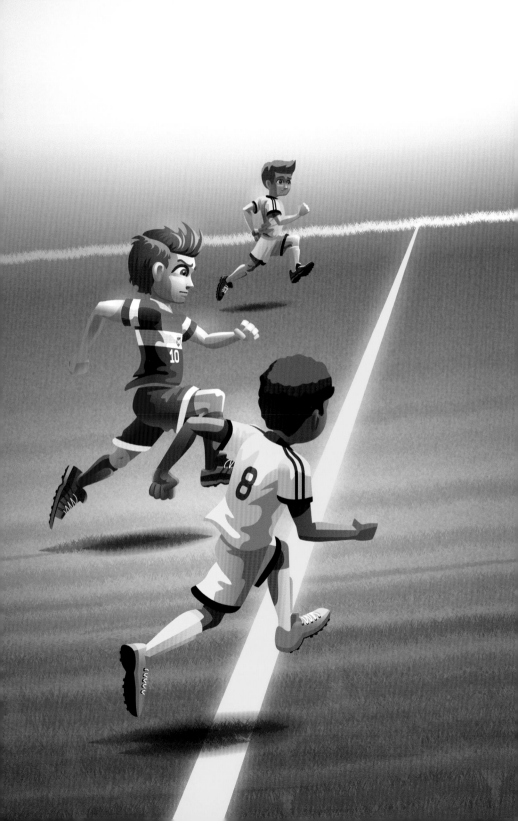

"Basically," Coach said, "you can't just hang out all alone behind the other team's defenders waiting for your team to pass the ball forward to you."

Boom! It finally clicked!

I can't just wait around behind the other teams' defenders hoping my teammates will pass the ball up the field to me. If I do that, I will be called offside. Instead, I need to start out level, or side by side, with the other team's defenders until my teammate kicks the ball forward!

To simplify the offside rule even more, Coach taught us that there are certain times in a game when we don't even need to worry about being in an offside position.

For example, he said we can never be offside in our own half of the field or on a throw in, goal kick, or corner kick. In any of these situations we should always feel free to run into space and even get behind the defense to create a scoring opportunity.

After Coach's halftime explanation about the offside rule, we only got "caught offside" a couple more times. Coach never got upset with us. He said that it was okay because we were trying to "play the line." Most teams get called offside at least a few times each game— even professionals!

After the game I was really proud because Coach said I did a great job of not getting "caught offside." Whenever my team had the ball, I made sure to look around at the other team's defenders and stay level with them until my teammates passed the ball to me.

I was so happy when we got through the defenders and scored a goal without the referee blowing his whistle to give the ball to the other team.

We tied our second game. Jaime scored the tying goal in the last minutes of the game. We did our cell phone selfie celebration we had secretly practiced that week. Coach yelled at us to hurry back to our positions and act like we've scored before, but he was smiling. Everybody was!

Teaching Concepts & Vocabulary

Offside: Found in FIFA Law 11, an offside offence occurs when an attacking player is in an offside position at the time the ball is played toward him and that player is subsequently involved in active play. If the infringement is enforced, the result is a stoppage of play and award of an indirect free kick to the non-offending team. Understanding the offside law requires understanding the concepts of offside position and active play.

Offside position: When an attacking player is positioned so that fewer than two opposing defensive players (usually the goalkeeper and 1 other defender) are between the attacking player and the goal he is attacking. The goalkeeper does not have to be included. The law focuses on whether the attacking player is nearer to the opponent's goal line than both the ball and the second to last defender. For example, if the Goalkeeper is advanced up-field beyond his defenders, an attacking player is in an offside position if the ball is played to him when there are fewer than two opposing players between himself and the goal.

Active play: Even when a player is in an offside position, he has not committed an offence until he becomes involved in "active play." Active play means interfering with play, interfering with an opponent or gaining an advantage from being in the offside position.

Interfering with an opponent: This broad term means preventing an opponent from playing or being able to play the ball. The referee may also rule that a player making a gesture or movement which deceives or distracts an opponent has interfered with that opponent. This determination is made at the discretion of the referee.

TIP: When you realize you have entered into an offside position but the ball is not yet played toward you, hurry back into an onside position and be ready for the next opportunity to attack!

TIP: It can be difficult for the referee to decide whether to enforce an offside infraction. Often, one of the teams will believe the referee has made a mistake. Nevertheless, players, coaches, and parents should always be kind and respectful to the referees. It is a challenging job, and we can't play an organized game without them!

Core Sources (From FIFA Laws of The Game 2014/15)

LAW 11 Offside Position: It is not an offence in itself to be in an offside position. A player is in an offside position if he is nearer to his opponents' goal line than both the ball and the second-last opponent.

A player is not in an offside position if (1) he is in his own half of the field of play or (2) he is level with the second-last opponent or (3) he is level with the last two opponents.

Offence: A player in an offside position is only penalized if, at the moment the ball touches or is played by one of his team, he is, in the opinion of the referee, involved in active play by (1) interfering with play or (2) interfering with an opponent or (3) gaining an advantage by being in that position.

No offence: There is no offside offence if a player receives the ball directly from (1) a goal kick, (2) a throw-in, (3) a corner kick.

Infringements and sanctions: In the event of an offside offence, the referee awards an indirect free kick to the opposing team to be taken from the place where the infringement occurred

Definitions (located in the interpretations of the laws of the game): In the context of Law 11 – Offside, the following definitions apply:

- "Nearer to his opponents' goal line" means that any part of a player's head, body or feet is nearer to his opponents' goal line than both the ball and the second-last opponent. The arms are not included in this definition.
- "Interfering with play" means playing or touching the ball passed or touched by a teammate.
- "Interfering with an opponent" means preventing an opponent from playing or being able to play the ball by clearly obstructing the opponent's line of vision or challenging an opponent for the ball.
- "Gaining an advantage by being in that position" means playing a ball (1) that rebounds or is deflected to him off the goalpost, crossbar or an opponent having been in an offside position, (2) that rebounds, is deflected or is played to him from a deliberate save by an opponent having been in an offside position.

  A player in an offside position receiving the ball from an opponent, who deliberately plays the ball (except from a deliberate save), is not considered to have gained an advantage.

EAT THE RIGHT THINGS!

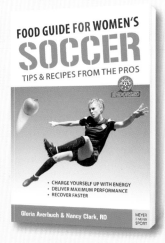

Averbuch/Clark, RD

FOOD GUIDE FOR WOMEN'S SOCCER

TIPS & RECIPES FROM THE PROS

Soccer players are hungry for good nutrition information. This easy-to-read book offers practical tips, debunks nutrition myths, and is a simple "how-to" resource for soccer players, their coaches and parents. Professional soccer players offer advice along with recipes and sample menus.

256 p., in color,

40 photos, 41 illus.,

paperback, 6 ½" x 9 ¼"

ISBN: 9781782550518

$ 18.95 US/$ 32.95 AUS

£ 14.95 UK/€18.95

All information subject to change © Thinkstock/ amana images

MOTIVATION AND FUN FOR YOUNG SOCCER PLAYERS

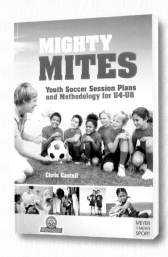

Chris Castell

MIGHTY MITES

YOUTH SOCCER SESSION PLANS AND
METHODOLOGY FOR U4-U8

Mighty Mites uses what we know about children and infuses this with soccer. Through stories, we engage young players in soccer. This approach helps coaches accomplish more whilst keeping every player engaged as they all have fun.

136 p., in color,
36 photos, 56 illus.,
paperback, 6 ½" x 9 ¼"

ISBN: 9781782550167

$16.95 US/$29.95 AUS
£12.95 UK/€16.95

MEYER & MEYER Sport
Von-Coels-Str. 390
52080 Aachen
Germany

Phone   +49 02 41 - 9 58 10 - 13
Fax   +49 02 41 - 9 58 10 - 10
E-Mail   sales@m-m-sports.com
Website   www.m-m-sports.com

All books available as E-books.

MEYER
& MEYER
SPORT

AN INFORMATIVE HANDBOOK FOR STREET SOCCER COACHES

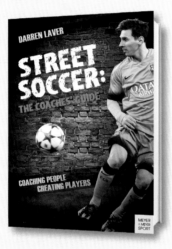

Darren Laver

STREET SOCCER: THE COACHES' GUIDE

COACHING PEOPLE, CREATING PLAYERS

This guide to street soccer coaching, written by the founder of the International Street Soccer Association (ISSA), is an informative, practical, and easy-to-use handbook for coaches of all levels. It contains 50 games— small sided and 1-v-1—that coaches can try out with their players in order to become more successful and still have fun.

176 p., in color,

c. 100 photos + illus.,

paperback, 6 ½" x 9 ¼"

ISBN: 9781782550518

c. $ 19.95 US/$ 30.95 AUS

£ 13.95 UK/€18.95

All information subject to change © Thinkstock/amana images

MEYER & MEYER Sport
Von-Coels-Str. 390
52080 Aachen
Germany

Phone   +49 02 41 - 9 58 10 - 13
Fax   +49 02 41 - 9 58 10 - 10
E-Mail   sales@m-m-sports.com
Website   www.m-m-sports.com

All books available as E-books.

MEYER
& MEYER
SPORT